This Book Belongs To:

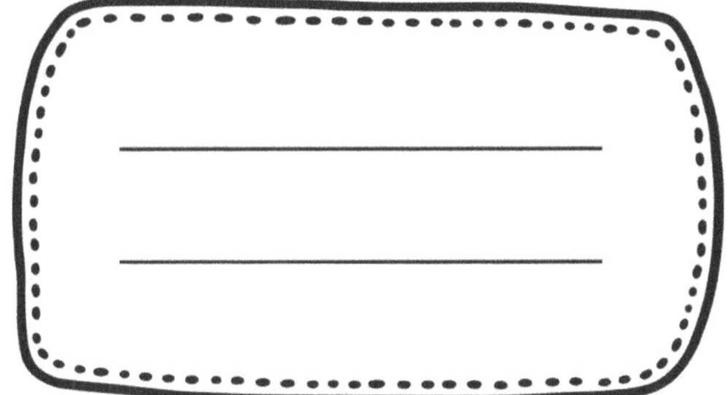

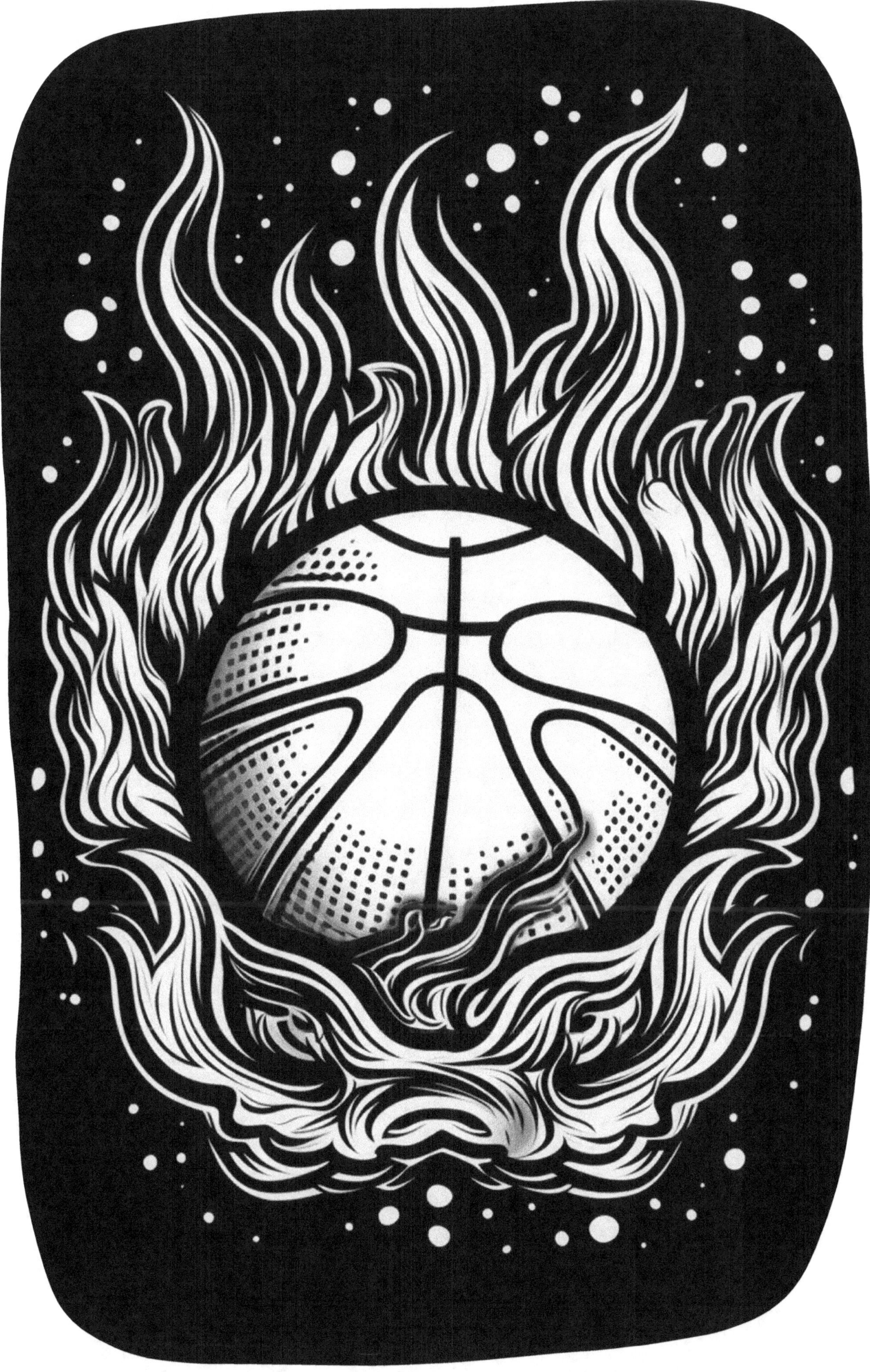

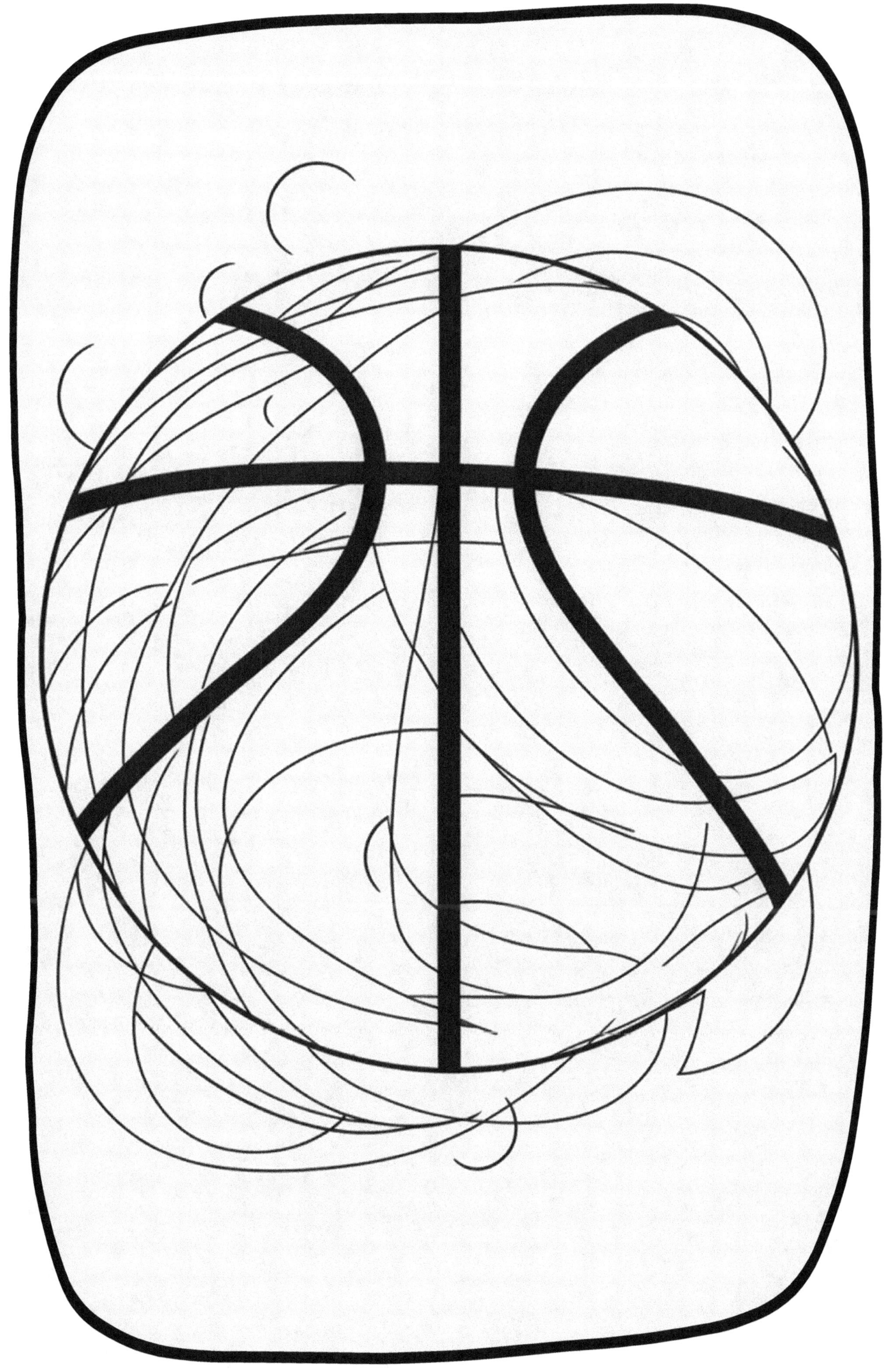

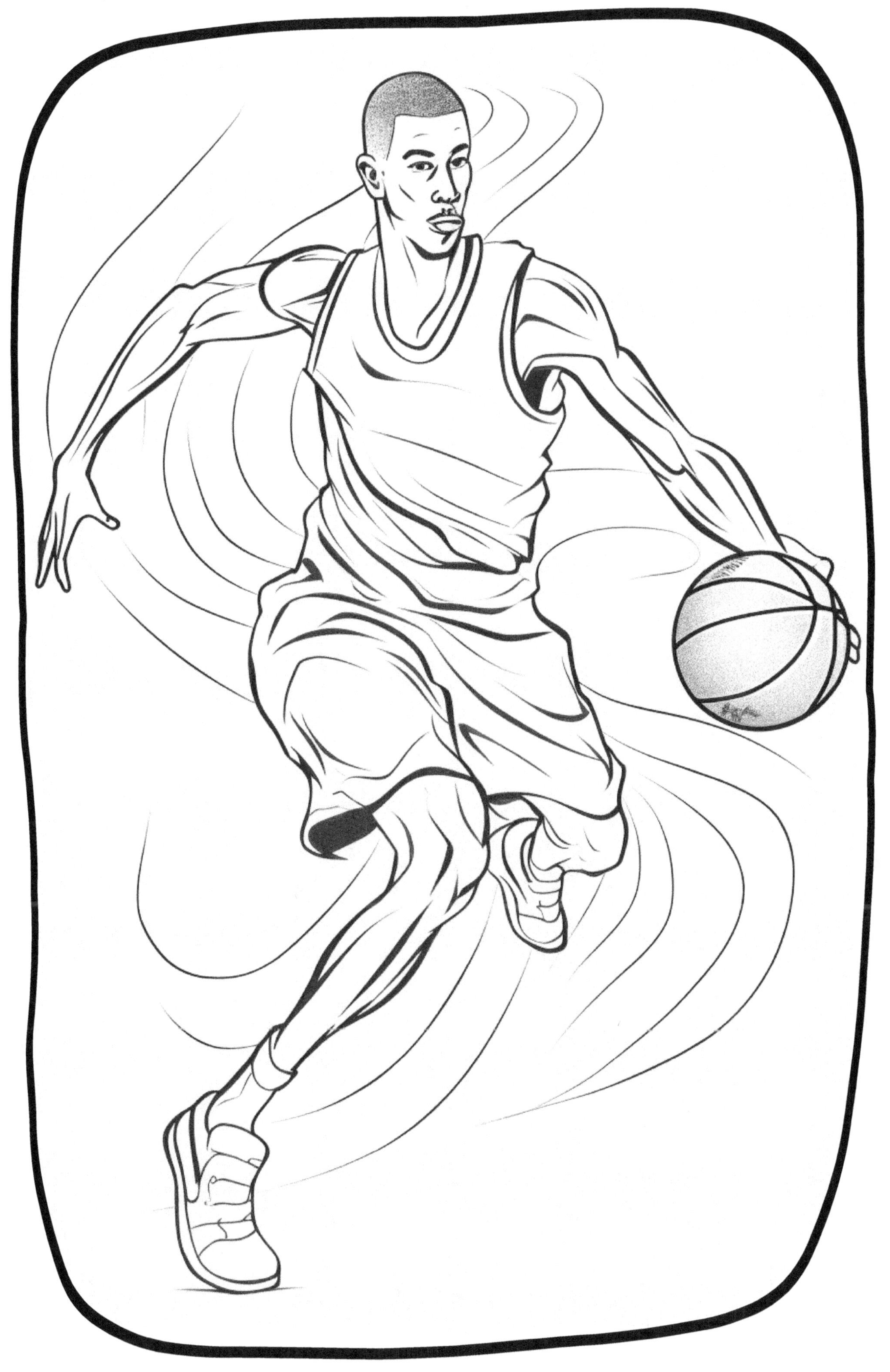

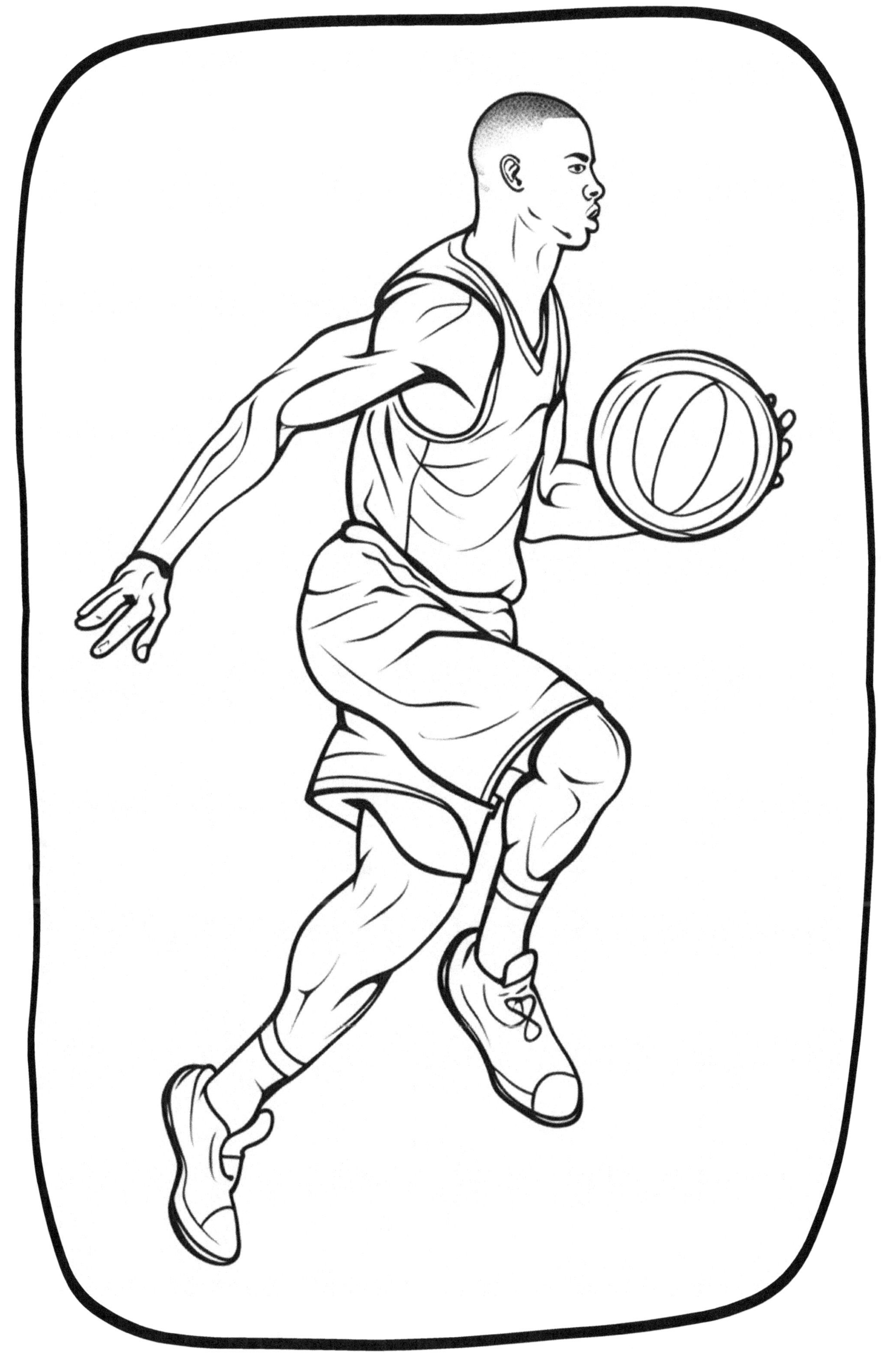

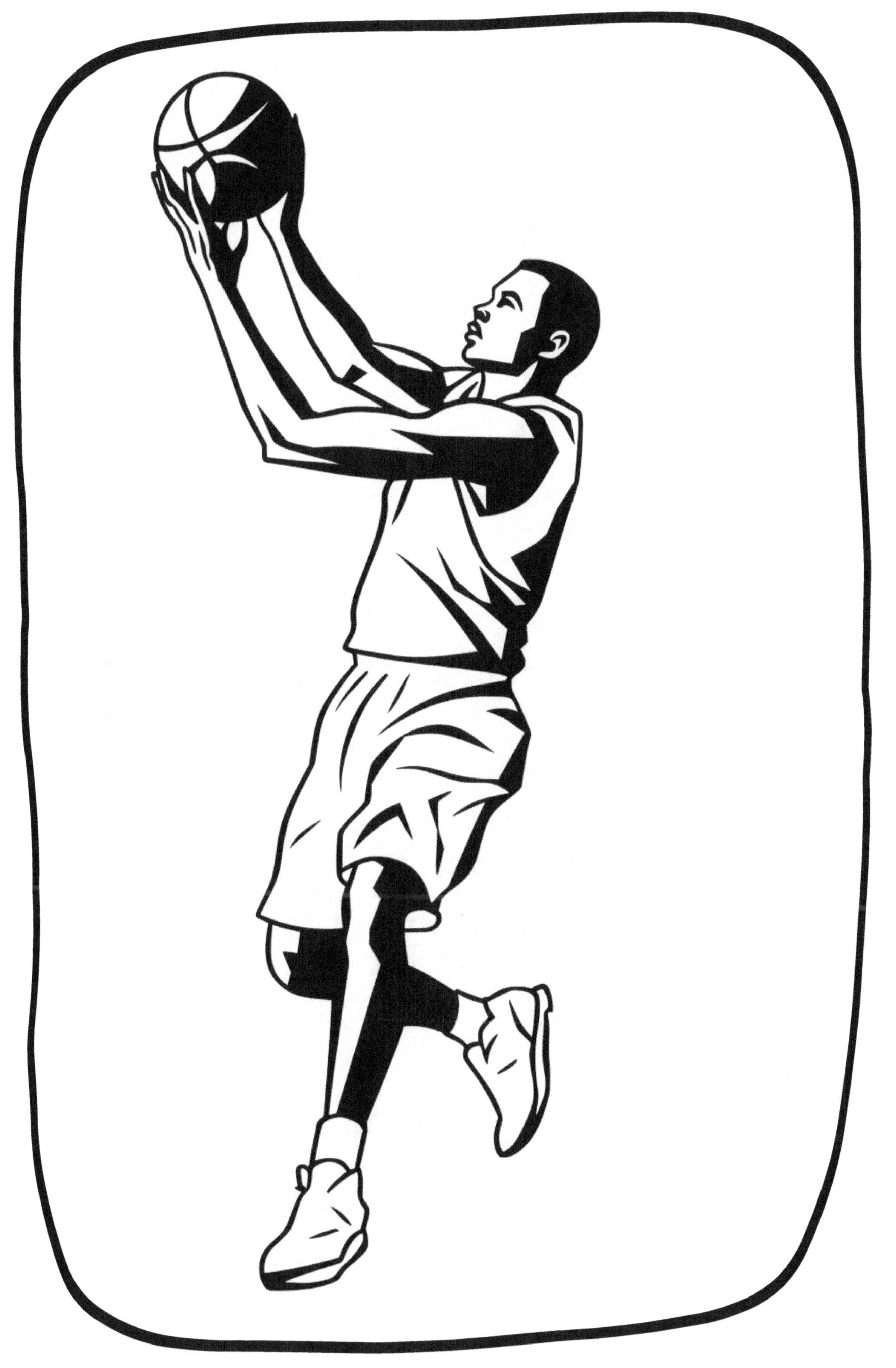

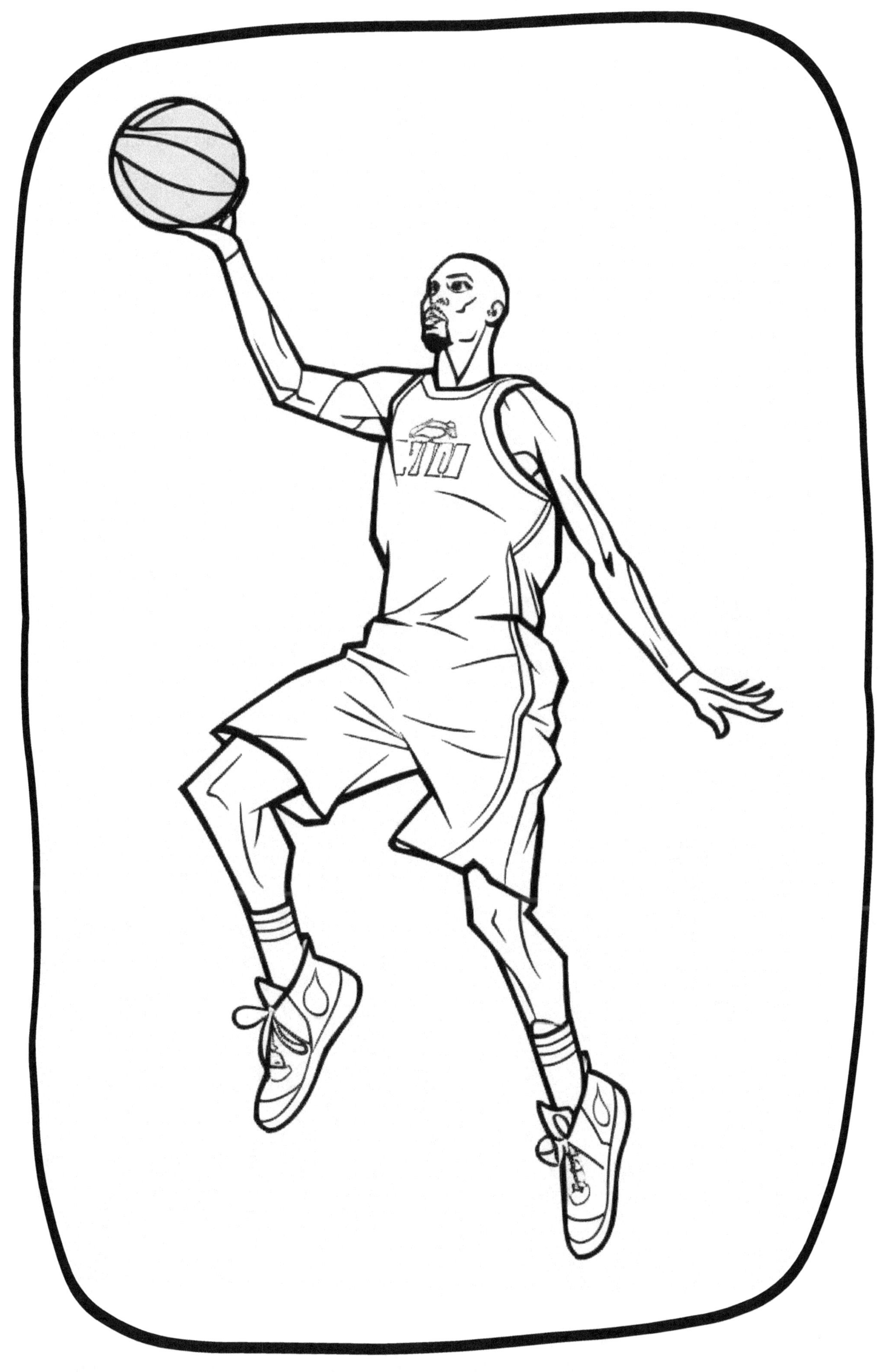

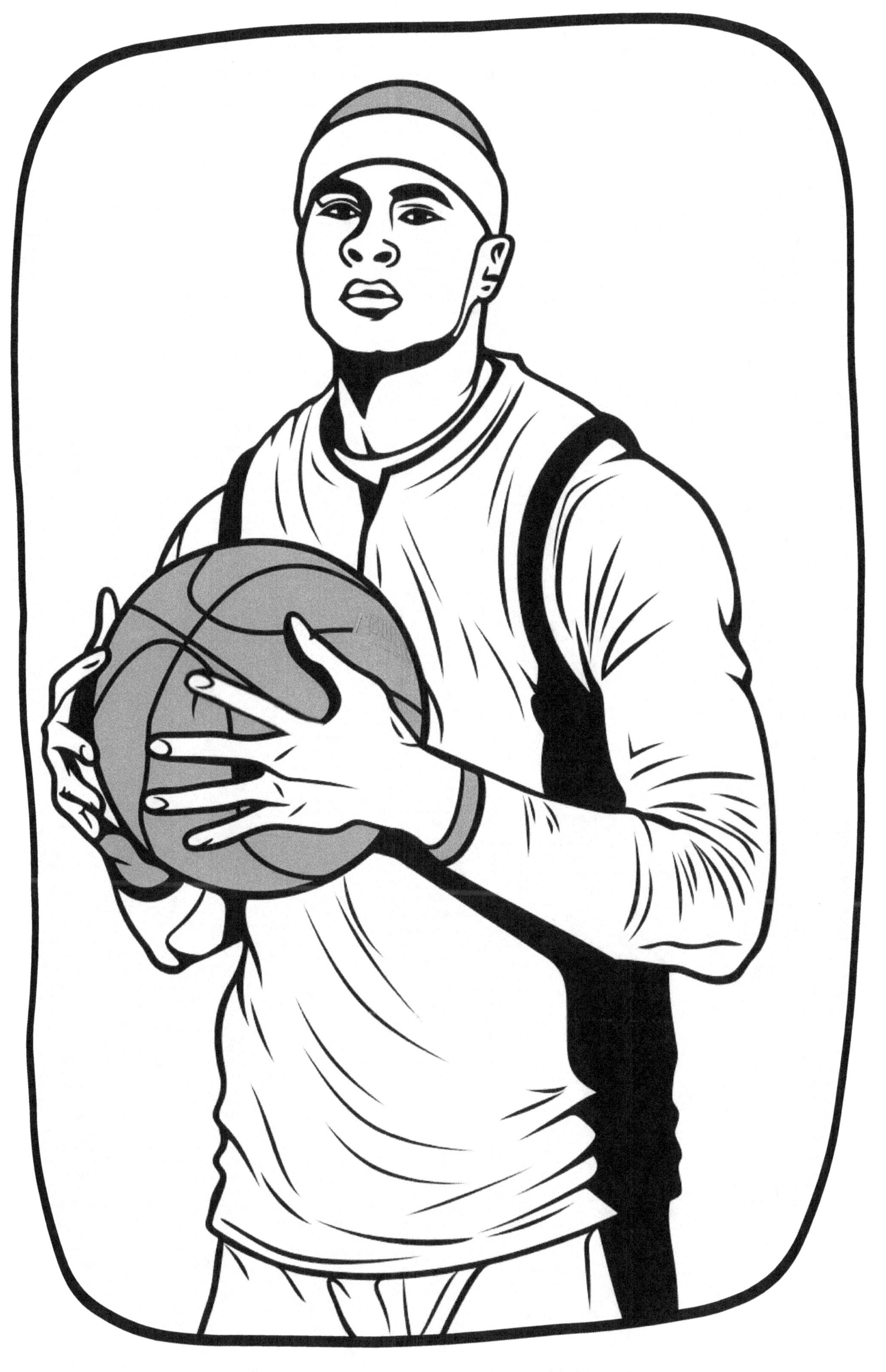

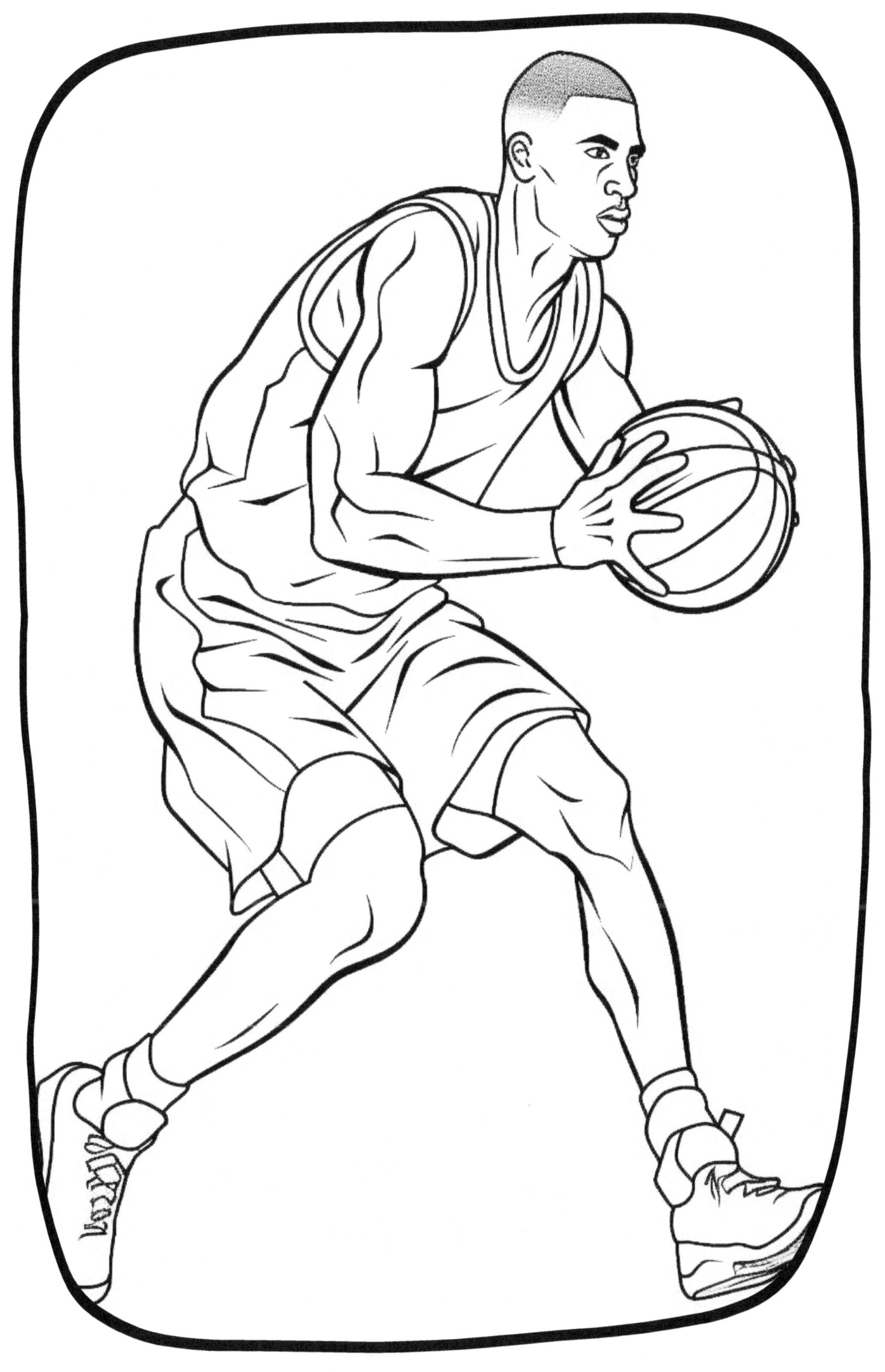

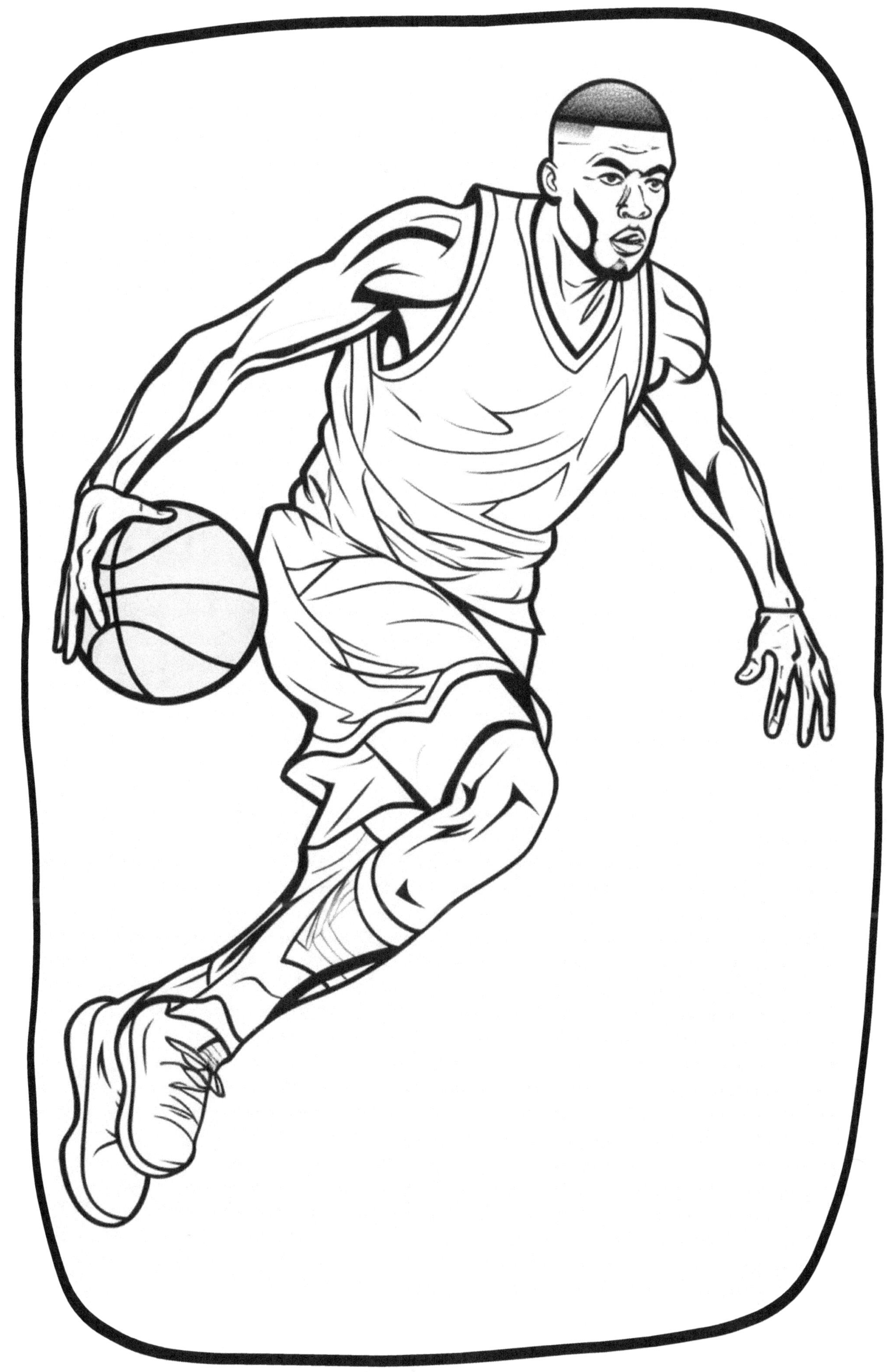

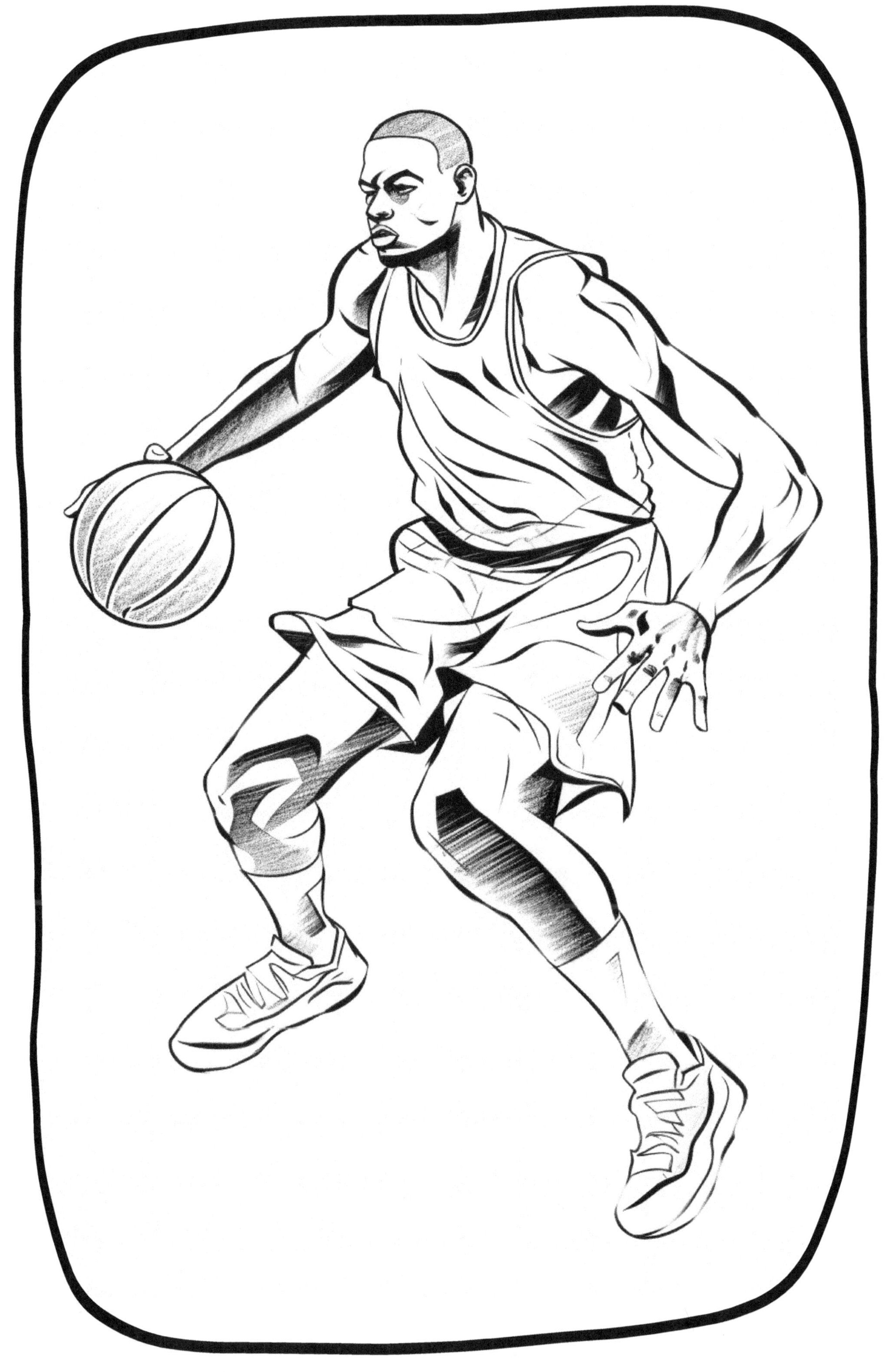

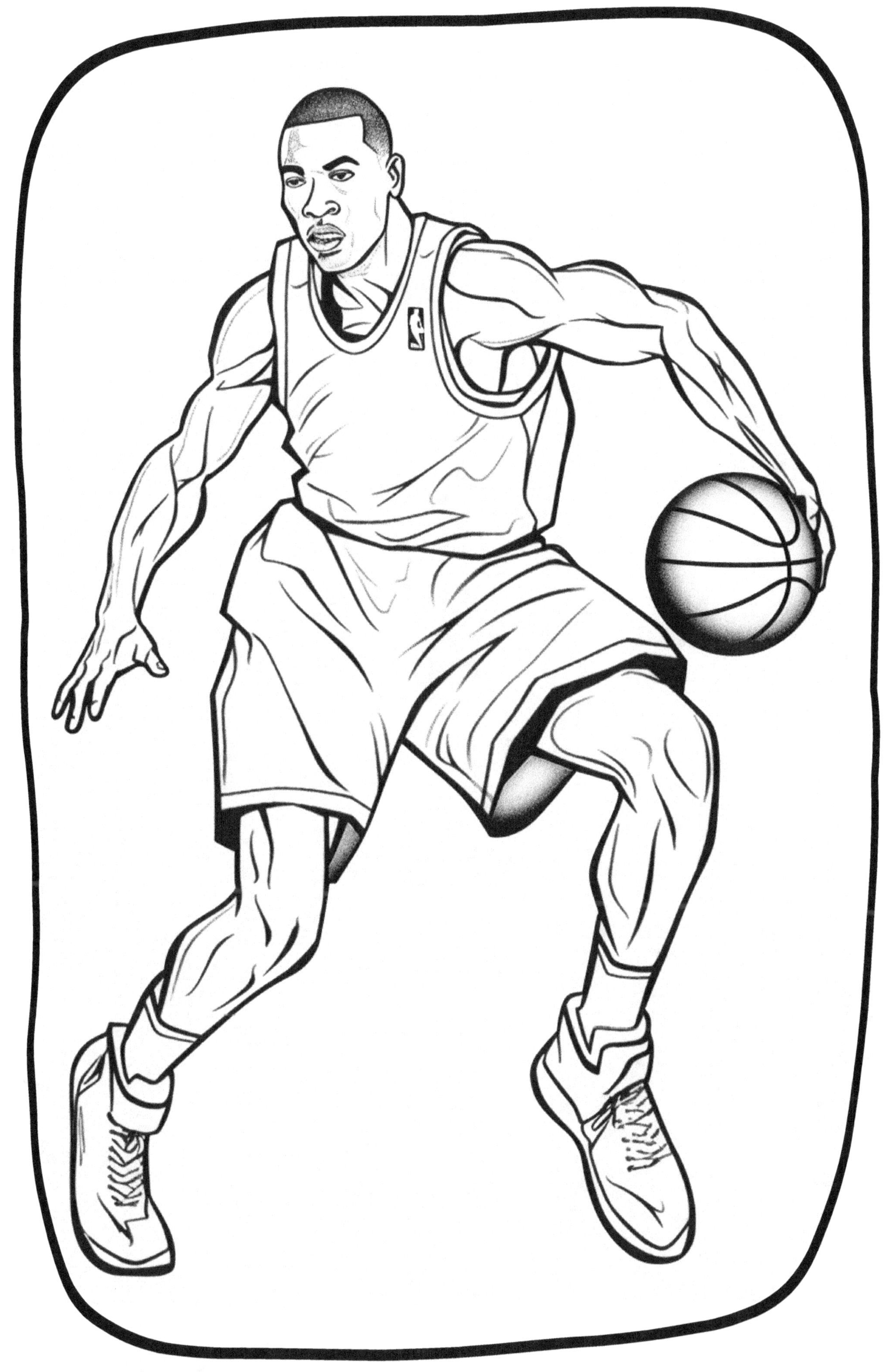

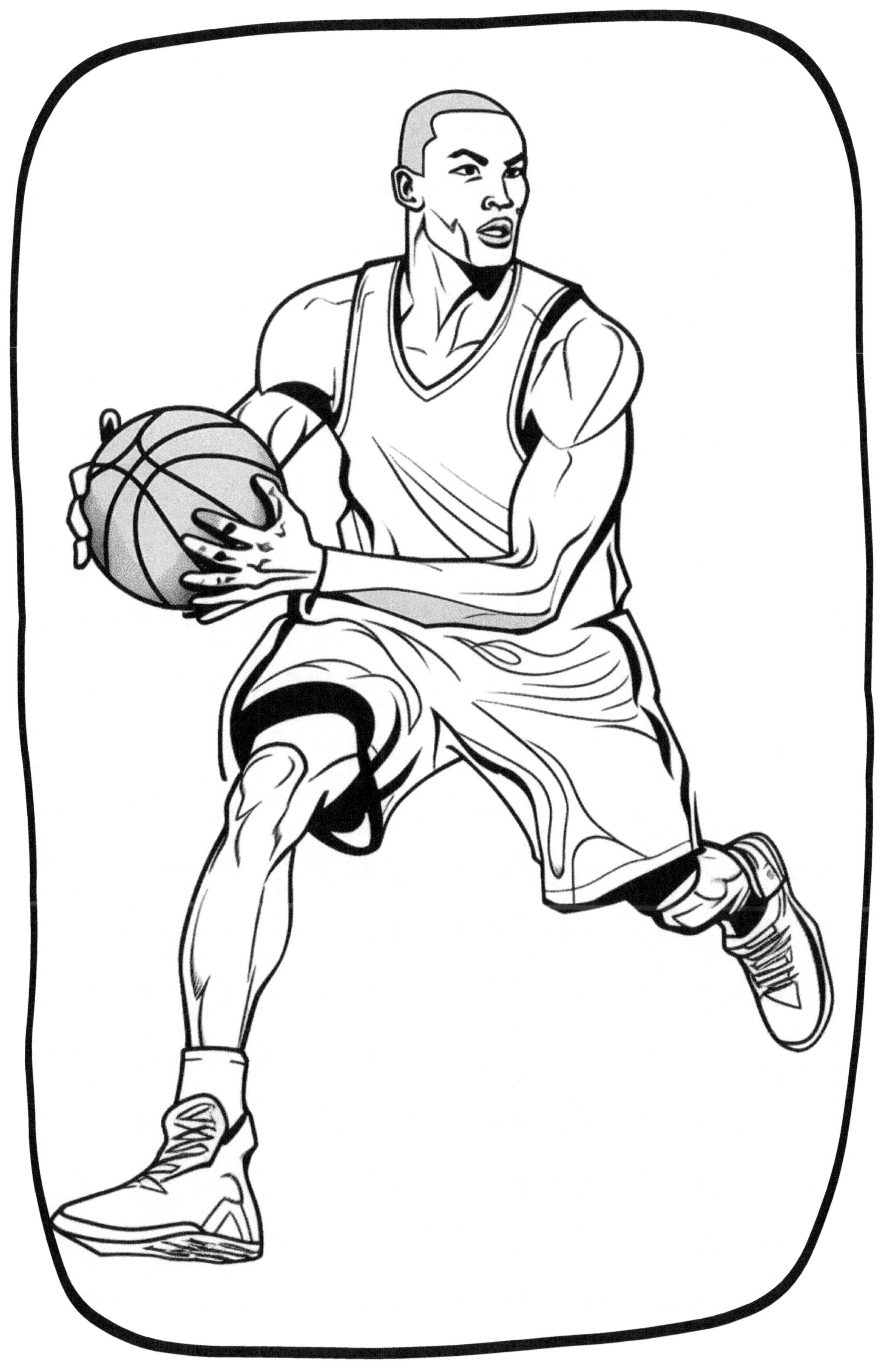

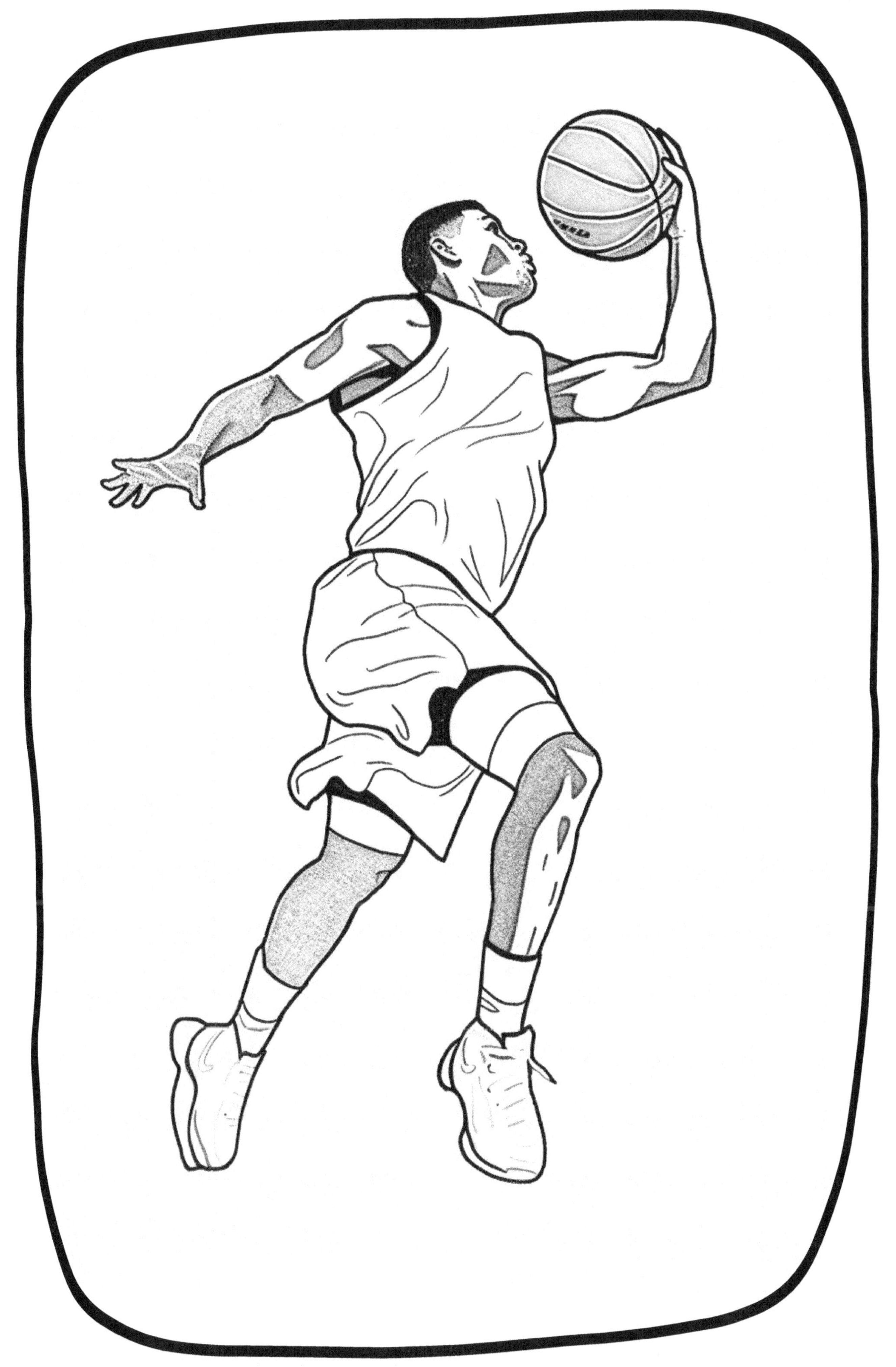

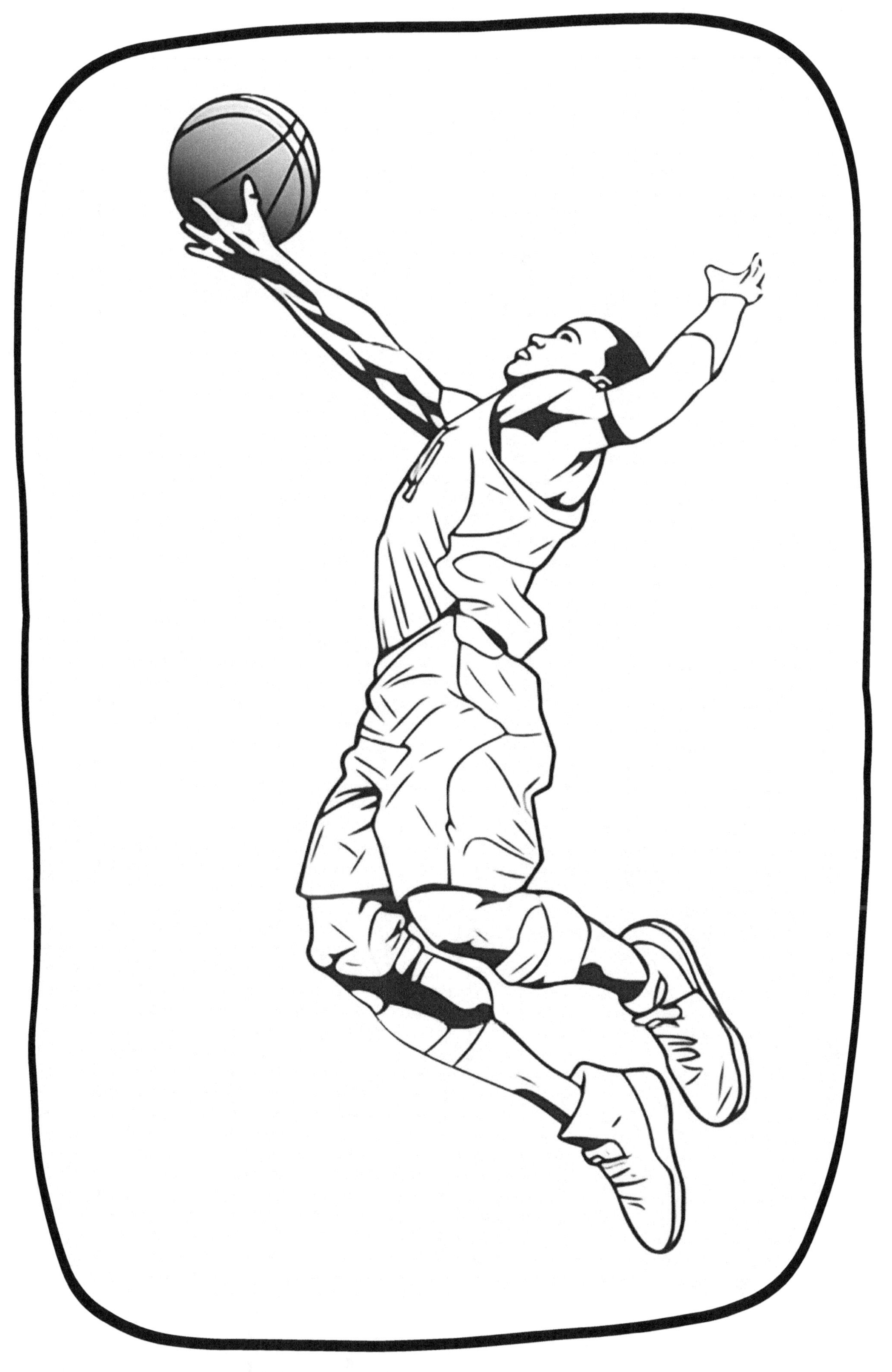

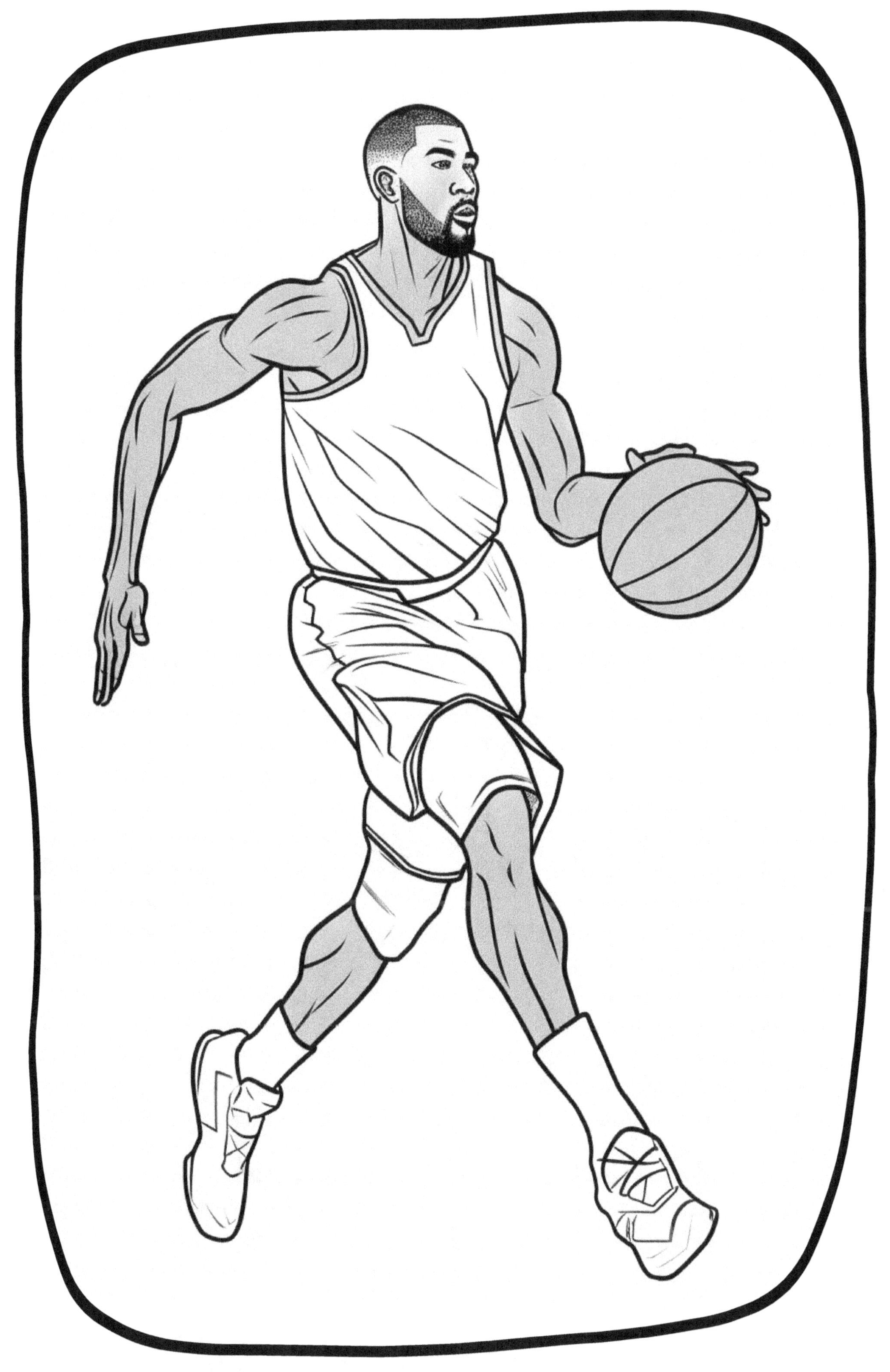

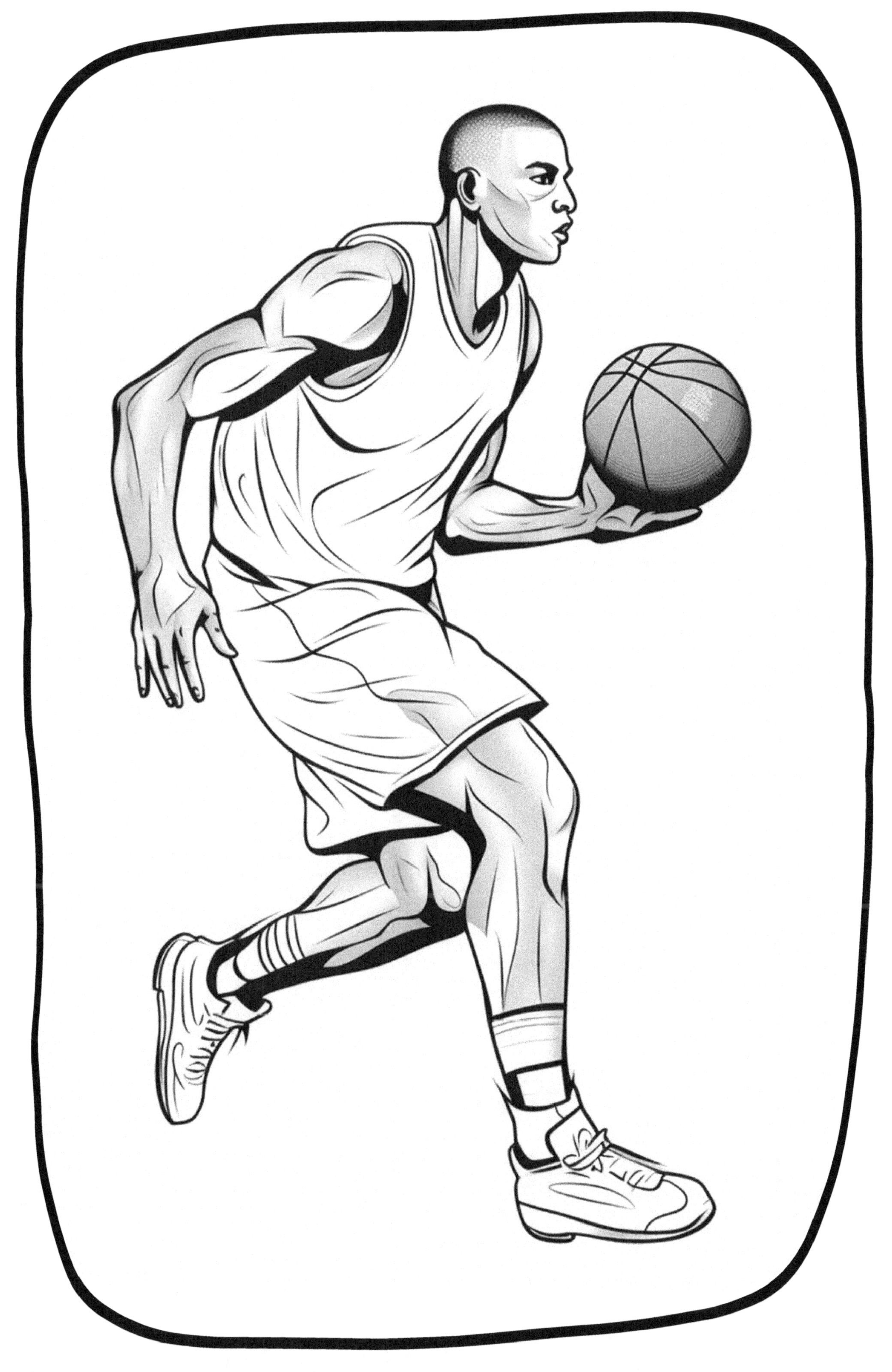

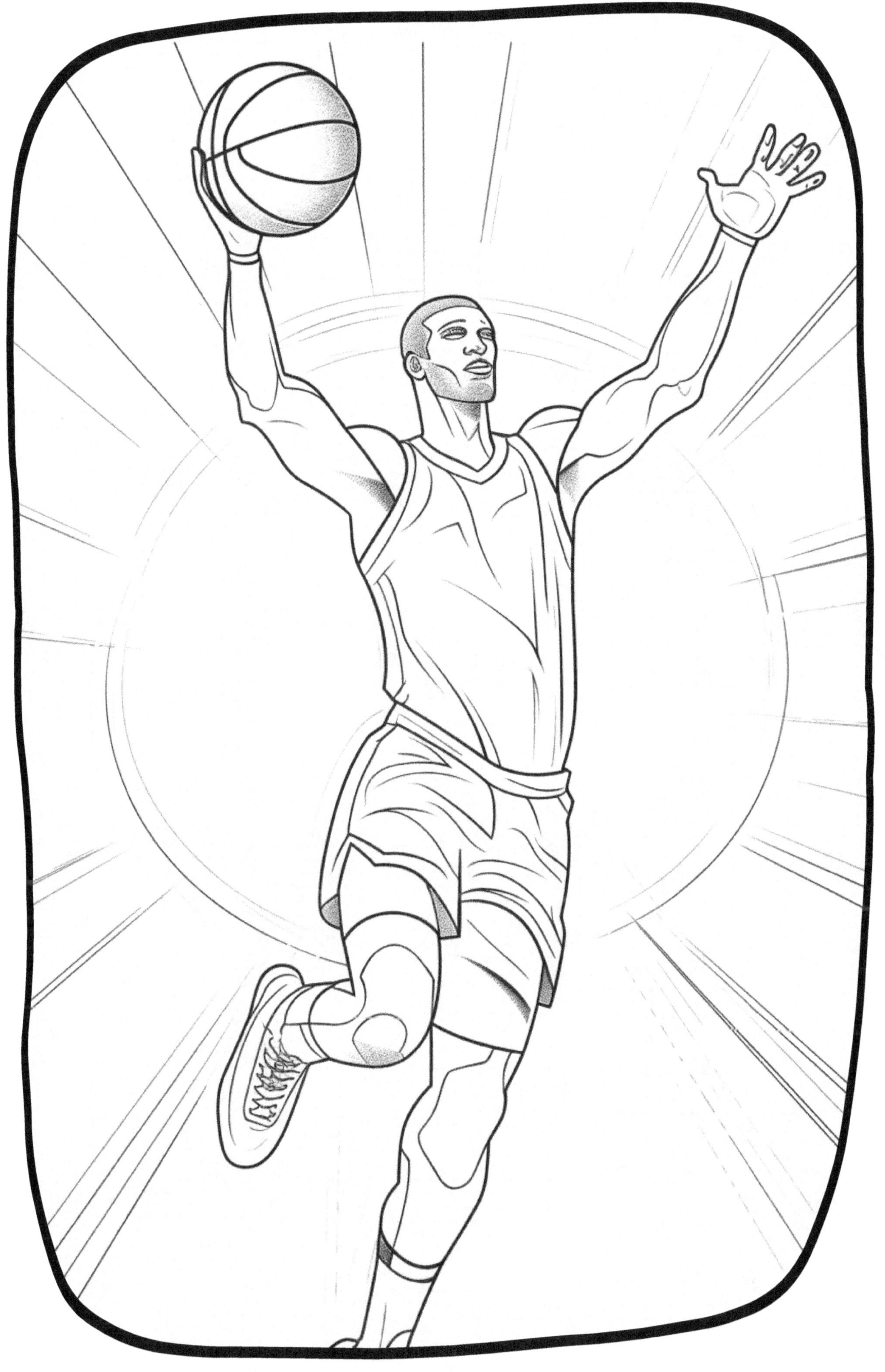

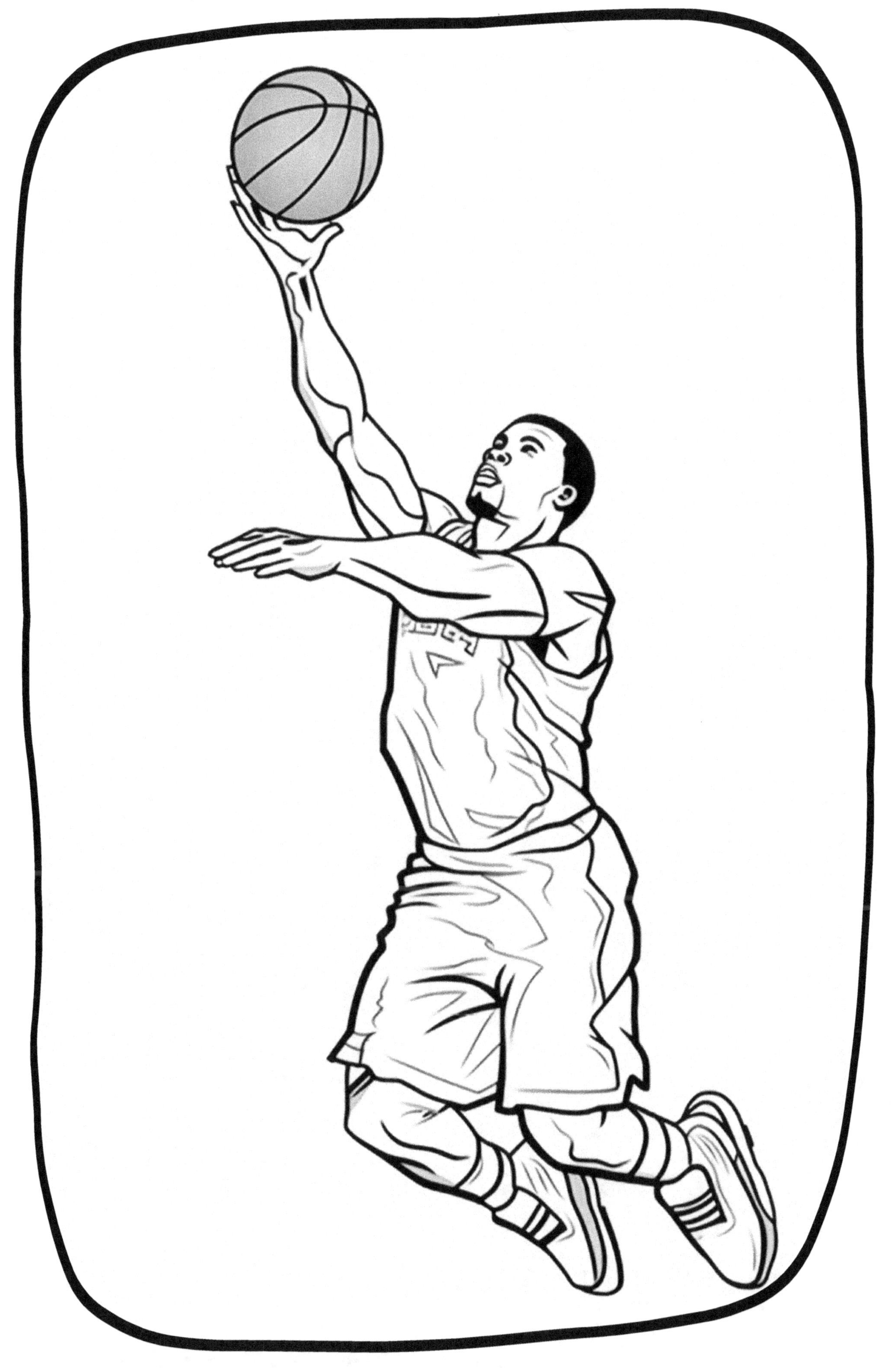

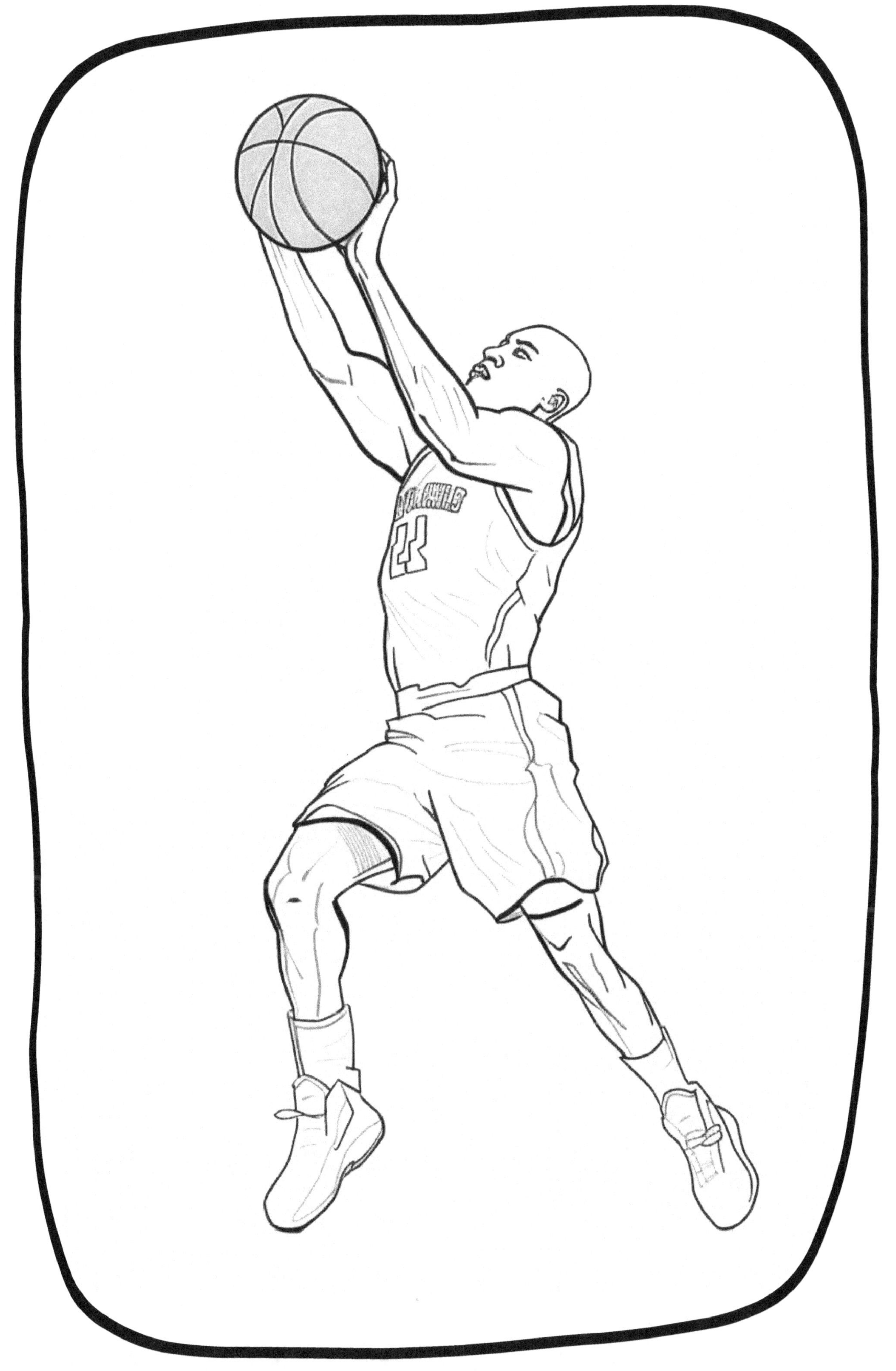
24

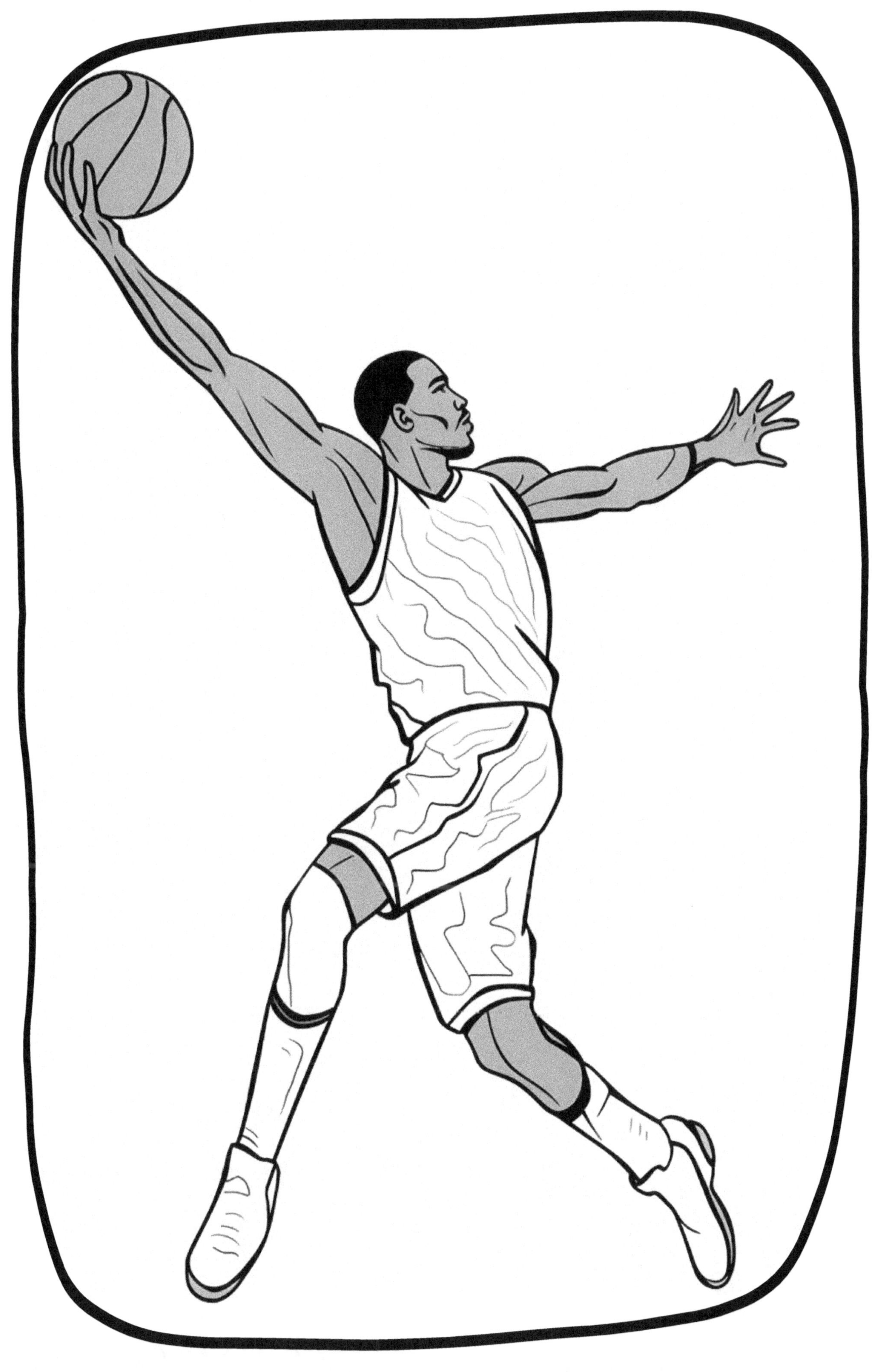

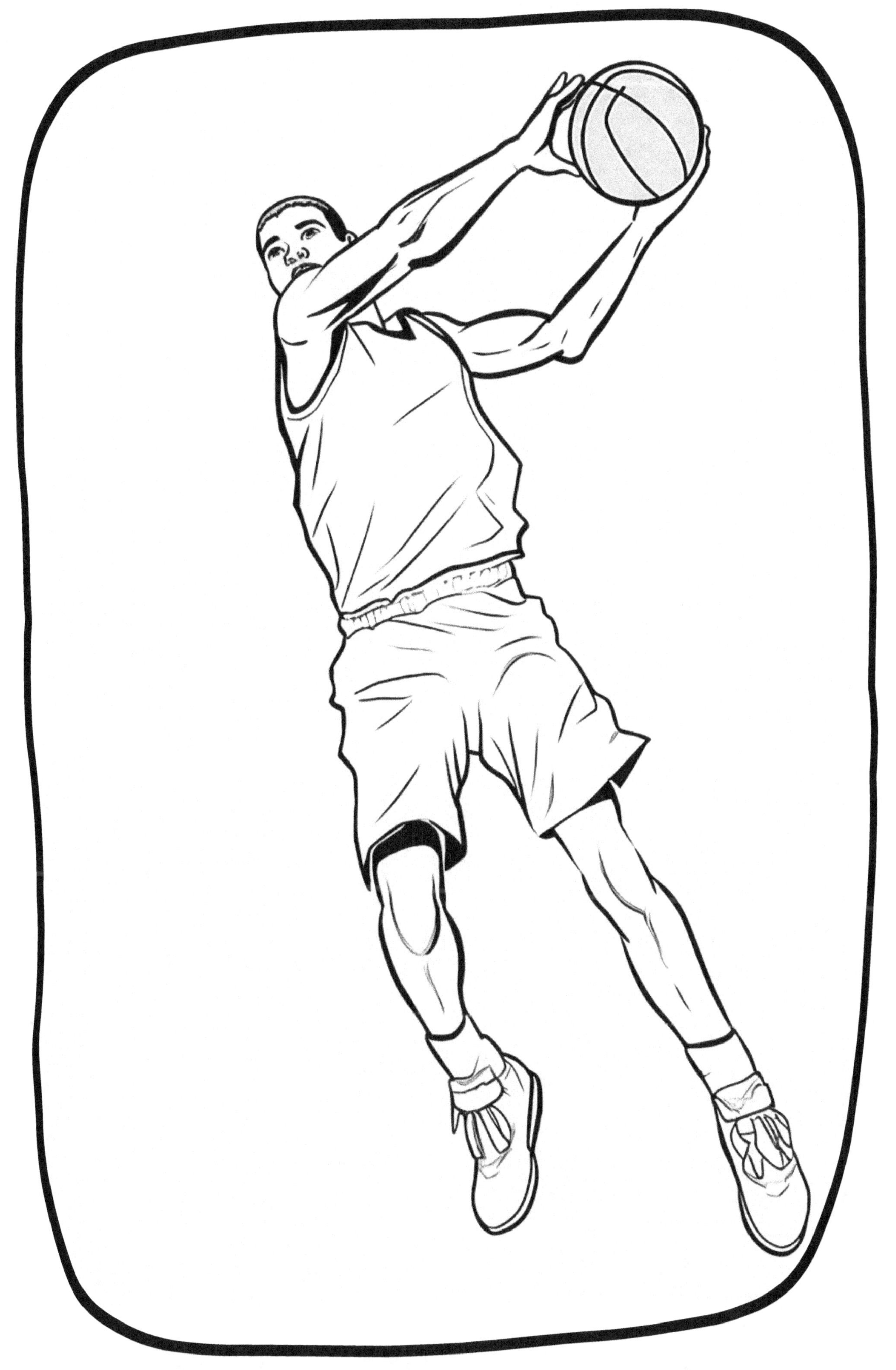

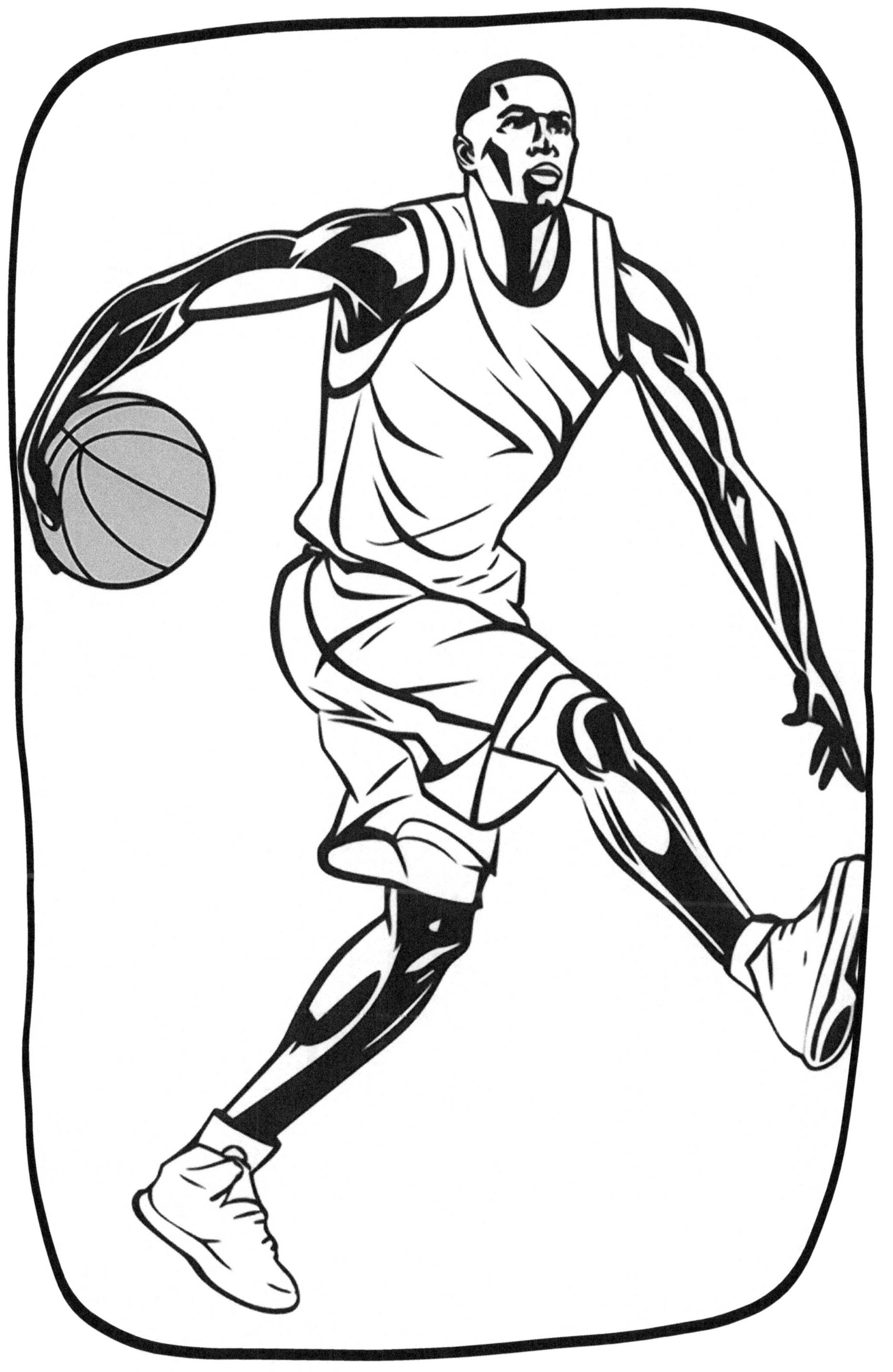

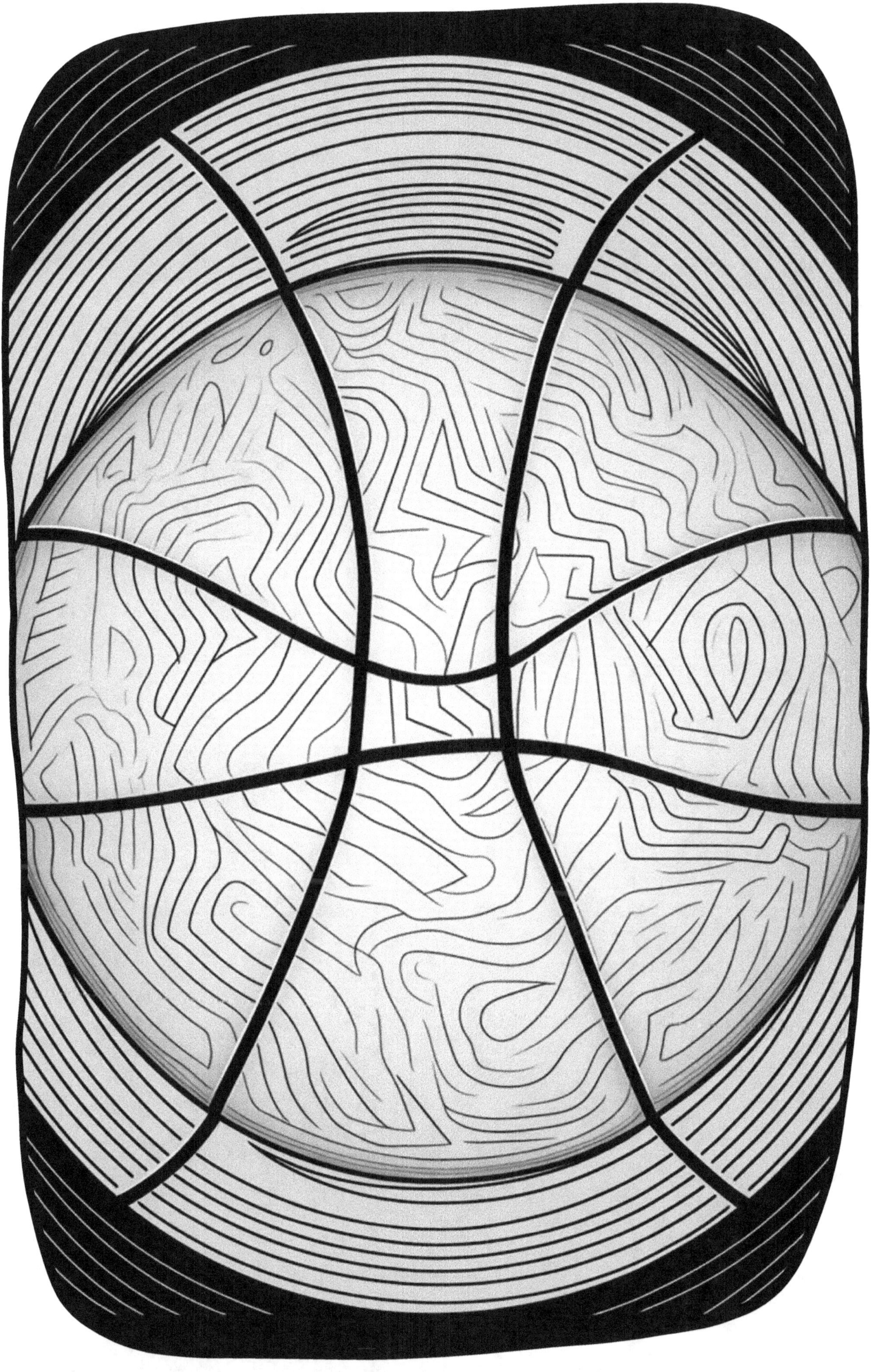

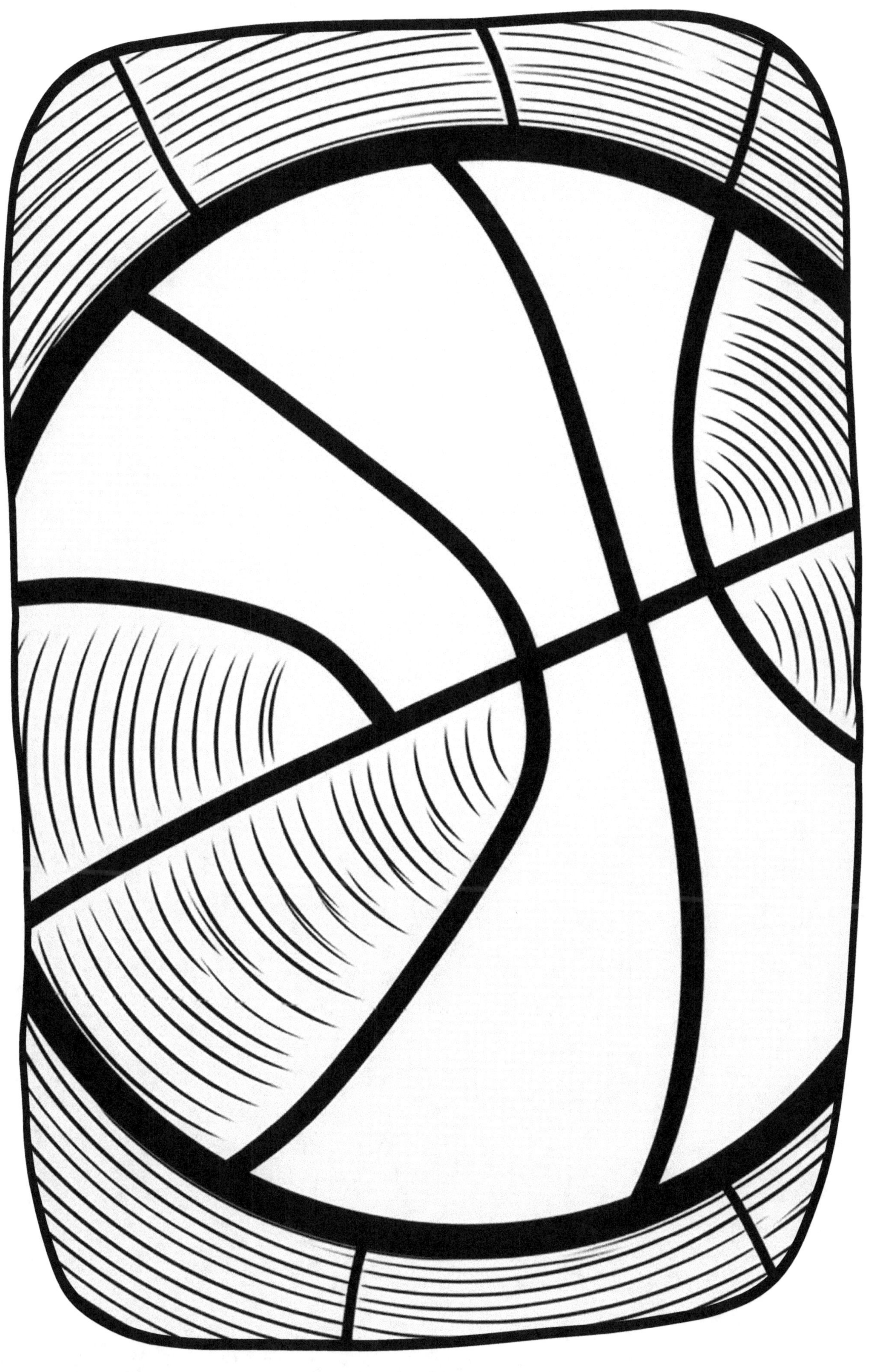

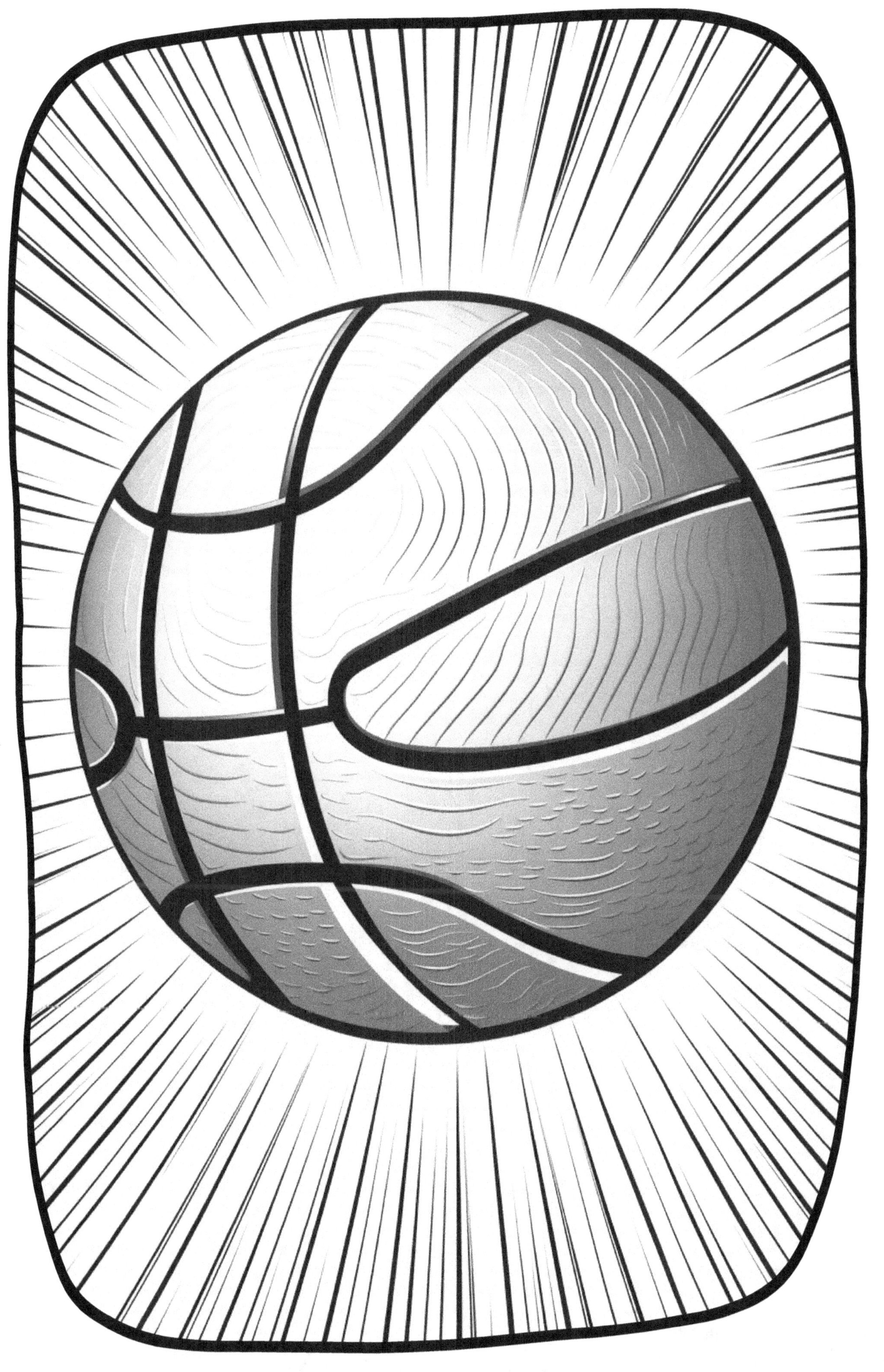